STOP
BEING LAZY!

How to Overcome Laziness, Defeat
Procrastination, Increase Productivity, and
Break Through Barriers Like an
Unstoppable Bulldog

TABLE OF CONTENTS

SECTION I

INTRODUCTION

CHAPTER 1

What this book is about

Several years ago, I created a blog (https://simpleprogrammer.com/sbl) and then a YouTube channel (https://simpleprogrammer.com/sbl-youtube) for software developers on a variety of challenges they face. I was covering software development issues, and started getting more and more requests for advice around life skills. For instance, I've gotten a ton of emails from people wanting dating advice. I remember getting one from a guy saying "I'm 21 and I've never had a girlfriend" and another from someone asking, "I'm going on a date, should I pay?" Out of all of the life skills issues that my community of followers bring up, the one that people are constantly asking me about is "how do I stop being so lazy?" Because the topic of laziness comes up quite a bit and because I, too, was lazy at one point in my life, I decided to share my journey and give practical advice by creating videos and blog posts on how to beat laziness. After realizing that this is a very painful struggle that most people have, I decided to explore this topic further and write this e-book. Laziness caused a lot of pain for me, but once I made the decision to just STOP, my life got so much better. No, it wasn't easy, and no I can't say that now my life is now pain free. The difference is that now I PROACTIVLELY and STRATEGICALLY chose my own pain. I don't let mediocrity or life problems kick my ass. I kick my own ass. I regularly pursue the empowering type of pain that builds strong character and strong muscles; muscles that are required for victory in any battle that life will inevitably throw my way. Kicking your own ass, which I'll explore more in this book, is a major cornerstone in breaking free from the bondage of laziness.

This book is divided into 5 sections. Section I gives you an overview of what the book is about and some insight into who I am, how I stopped being lazy and became, what I call, a bulldog. Section II is all about mindset. If you don't have an empowering mindset, you won't be an empowered person and you will therefore not act in a powerful way. You will continue to be a lazy ass. The saying, I think, therefore I am speaks volumes. If you think you are lazy, your actions and your life will reflect the fruits of laziness. If you think you're a fucking bulldog, you will take action, whether you feel like it or not, and get shit done—CONSISTENTLY, in EVERY area of your life. And yes, your life will see the fruits of being a bulldog, which consists of more muscle, more confidence, more productivity, and a life as you define it. Section III is about changing your actions. Once your mind is changed to an empowered state— the state of a bulldog—you will need practical strategies to CONTINUOUSLY CRUSH IT. In this section, I share some powerful strategies that support my bulldog mindset. Section IV is all about moving forward in your journey. You don't want to fall into a pattern of laziness again after, say, a month of hard work. When you become a fucking bulldog, it is an unbelievable feeling and just the thought of going back to being a lazy sap will cause you excruciating pain. So, you must keep moving forward. Not letting life move you forward, but you must continue on the path that you started and take life by the horns and move life forward in the direction YOU want to go. Section V is the conclusion. Here, I wrap things up and invite you to sign-up for a free resource I created called The *Bulldog's Playlist (https://simpleprogrammer.com/bulldog-playlist). The Bulldog's Playlist* is a short companion resource that's meant to help you on your journey out of laziness. In it, I recommend books, blogs, podcasts, and other resources to help you stay focused. One of the things I will get into in the mindset section (specifically in the chapter on Establishing a new regime), is controlling your inputs. I'll go into more detail in that section, but what goes into your mind determines your nature and your character. Just like you are what you eat...you are the media you consume. Today, far too many people's characters are being determined by mainstream media. Choose your own media. Read and listen to things that will set you up for success and keep you on the path of being a bulldog.

Now, let's get started! Get ready to rip off the seatbelt of laziness and become an unbridled fucking bulldog that gets what he or she wants out of life.

CHAPTER 2

My Story—How I stopped being lazy and became a bulldog

8 years ago, I was working in a cubicle as a contractor in Idaho. I had a good job, but compared to now, my life was pretty average. I was overweight. I didn't have nearly as much muscle as I have now. I ate a lot of junk. I didn't have a fitness routine. I had very little self-confidence or self-esteem. The confidence I did have was rooted in arrogance. I was a very fearful person and even had panic attacks. Compared to my life today, I was very lazy. I had no dream and no vision for my life. I had no ambition of being an entrepreneur. In fact, like most people, I was getting up and going to work every day and when I came home, I watched TV and maybe played some video games. I have transformed my life so much that I don't even recognize who I was and I can't even imagine living like that again. What I talk about, what I think about, and the way I carry myself has completely changed. Today, I'm much more outgoing. I have developed my voice and my personality so much more. I'm a lot more confident and my self-esteem has increased tremendously. I now read a ton of personal development books, and back then, I hadn't read very many books at all. I have overcome my fears and I can proudly say that I am not lazy. How did I do all of this? I DECIDED to stop being lazy and become a fucking bulldog so that I could get what I wanted from life. I was tired of watching other people succeed and

feeling like I was waiting for my turn. I was tired of waiting for "someday", which, for me, never came. I came to the realization that I needed to be tenacious. I had to stop being complacent in life and figure out how to get what I wanted. I didn't want to be that average guy anymore. I wanted to be the fucking best at whatever I wanted to pursue. And I wanted the rewards for being the best. I started my transformation by just visualizing who I wanted to become. I stepped into the shoes of this better version of myself. But I didn't stop there. Merely having a vision for your life doesn't make you a bulldog. The first thing that made me a bulldog is having a vision of the life I wanted and holding onto that vision no matter what. I realized that I had to plough through shit. I had to become a finisher no matter what the obstacles were. I had to finish shit that I didn't want to do. The second thing I did to become a fucking bulldog was to do hard shit. Not only are bulldogs tenacious, they have muscle. What builds muscle? Doing hard shit. Challenging yourself and pushing yourself to do what you think is impossible builds mental toughness. And if the hard shit you decide to do is physical, then you will also build physical muscles. This is important because life always throws challenges at us. And when we challenge ourselves before life does, we are better able to beat those challenges. Bulldogs are not lazy. They can't be. They are always moving forward, plowing through shit. The only cure for laziness is forward motion. When resistance comes with forward motion, you build muscle and get stronger, making you ready for the next challenge. This is how I stopped being lazy and became a fucking bulldog.

CHAPTER 3:

You too, can be a bulldog—Here's how

Think of a celebrity, an athlete, or maybe just someone you know, who is a bulldog as I described in the last chapter. Someone who's living the kind of life you dream about. The person who is fearless, goes after what they want, makes shit happen, and is NOT lazy. How do you think they got to where they are? Actually, a better question is...how do you think they BECAME WHO they are? Do you think they're smarter than you, luckier than you, more attractive than you, more athletic than you, more...fill in the blank than you? I'm sure you've heard people say things like, I'm no Steve Jobs, or you're no pick your favorite celebrity, as if celebrities or people you admire have some kind of magic power that you don't. I'm here to tell you that is absolute bullshit. The only difference between you and them comes down to one thing. And that one thing is...a DECISION. That's right, a decision. They DECIDED they were going to live life on their terms. They DECIDED to crush laziness. They DECIDED to be fearless. They DECIDED to live proactively instead of reactively. They DECIDED to say fuck you to mediocrity and do hard shit that would build muscles of courage and resilience. That's the difference. Once you make a decision, a real decision that you are 100% committed to, **your mindset will change**. And our mindsets reflect the decisions we make. When we change our mindset, we become different people. When you become a different person, you act like this new person that you've decided to become. So you see, these celebrities or athletes, or gurus really are no different from you. You are where you are right now because of decisions that you've made. Your decisions have shaped your mindset. And your mindset is now dictating your actions, which has you in the state of laziness and fear instead of where you really want to be. Just 8 years ago, I was right where you are. Lazy and living in fear. If you haven't already, you can check out my YouTube channel (https://simpleprogrammer.com/sbl-youtube) and see my progression over the years and how my life has drastically changed for the better. The only difference between you and me is the decision that I made 8 years ago to become a bulldog and go after the life I deserve and become the person I wanted to become. There are people I knew 8 years ago who have not changed much at all, other than being older and fatter. And the difference between me and them is that I made a different decision and you can clearly see the results.

So...how can YOU stop being lazy and become a bulldog that gets the life you want and deserve? DECIDE! Just make the decision. There's an old saying that goes, "when the student is ready, the teacher will appear". If you are ready—which only requires you to make the decision—I will be your teacher. I'm gonna teach you how to take a really hard bite of what you want out of life. I will inspire you to really sink your teeth in — and hold onto that shit no matter what obstacles or other bullshit comes your way. Does that sound good? Do you want to stop being lazy and be a fucking bulldog? Good. Let's do it then.

SECTION II

CHANGE YOUR MINDSET

CHAPTER 4

Start a fucking revolution...in your mind

Before I get into starting a revolution in your mind, I want to talk to you about what usually happens before a revolution. A revolution usually begins with a strong vision or desire for a life or a society that is different from how that society is currently living. Think about what happens in an uprising. The faction that's trying to overthrow an established regime has a vision for a life that conflicts with the vision of the regime in power. They know that a revolution will be hard, and what keeps them going is a strong vision of what life could be like if there was a change in leadership. And let's not forget, the regime in power will not gladly hand over the keys to the kingdom just because the opposition wants them to. In fact, they will fight to the death to stay in power. This is what happens when you start a revolution in your mind. Your current regime, which is laziness and mediocrity, will fight to keep the same mindset and the same habits that result in your current life. It's not that your current mindset is trying to harm you in any way. It's actually quite the opposite. It's trying to protect you from pain. The pain of experiencing the hard shit that is required of making a real change and becoming a bulldog. To get you through those times you want to quit, throw in the towel and go back to the land of mediocrity, your vision has to be powerful, clear, and compelling enough to drive you to keep going, to keep moving forward even if it hurts like hell. That's why, before you start a revolution in your mind, you must have a powerful vision. A vision of the bigger and better life you want to live and of the stronger and more powerful person you want to become. So how do you create this powerful vision? Use your imagination. Really visualize and experience what it feels like to be this bad ass version of yourself that can do the impossible. Think big. Dream big. Imagine doing some bad ass shit you never thought you were capable of. Ask yourself what does the life you want look like? What does it feel like? Really put yourself there, in the shoes of your future self, your higher self, your better self. In your imagination, really be this person you want to become. Hold onto that vision when you're doing something hard and you want to give up. When you have this compelling vision, don't ever let it go. Make revisions and make it better so that you are always moving forward, but don't ever let it go. Be tenacious and hold on to it through all the bullshit that life throws at you and that you will throw at yourself on this journey to becoming a bulldog. With this powerful vision burned into your psyche, you are now ready to start a fucking revolution. It's time for you to blow some shit up…in your mind.

With a powerful vision in hand, you are now ready to start your revolution. Always remember, the revolution of your mind will not happen in one day or with one act of courage. The revolution of your mind will take place over time. And eventually, the old regime of laziness will be wiped out. One of the first things you need to do on this journey is to stop associating yourself with being lazy and start associating yourself with being a bulldog. Yes, STOP saying that you are lazy. Say to yourself, "yesterday I was lazy, but today, I am a fucking bulldog!" Even if you don't quite feel like a bulldog yet, say it anyway. This may sound like some new age shit, but who the hell cares?? This shit works. In the words of motivational speaker, Les Brown, "Your subconscious is always listening." And it's true. Your subconscious mind does what you tell it to do, and if you tell it that you're lazy, you will be lazy. You must change your nature and your self-belief. If you believe you're something, you will prove yourself right. How we perceive ourselves lays the groundwork for the person we become. Constantly telling myself that I am a bulldog works for me, and it can work for you too! Another thing to remember about beliefs is that they don't have to be entirely true. They just need to be effective. And, right now, you need to believe that you are not lazy and that you are a bulldog, so keep telling yourself that no matter what. This is a critical part of your revolution. You are uprooting the lazy mindset by not associating your identity with it. By doing this everyday throughout the day, your identity and who you perceive yourself to be will change. This is the moment the revolution begins. When you perceive yourself as a different person, as a bulldog, you have won a very important battle and have laid the groundwork for victory.

In order to make your new identity of being a bulldog more real and to put even more distance between yourself and your old identity of being lazy, you must take action…actions of a bulldog. I will go into more detail on taking action in Section III, but I am addressing it here because taking action right away is so important in establishing your new mindset. At this point, right at the beginning, you must do something that this new version of yourself would do. When you have a mindset shift, in order to keep it, you must act immediately. What type of actions should you take? Let's go back to the vision of the better life you want or this better, more powerful person you want to become. Is this version of you lean, fit, and energetic? If yes, then go to the fucking gym and work out. Is this new version of yourself more outgoing and confident? Then get your ass off the couch and go to a party and make it your mission to talk to everyone there, even if the old you would be too afraid or too lazy to take the lead in starting conversations. Does the bulldog you get more shit done and is more productive? Then go out, find productivity tools and techniques, and USE them. I have a list of productivity tools and techniques in The *Bulldog's Playlist* resource that can give you some ideas. Download this free guide here (https://simpleprogrammer.com/bulldog-playlist). Don't just read about them or watch YouTube videos, get some tools and use them to achieve a goal the new bulldog you wants to achieve. When you take this type of action, you are confirming to your subconscious that you really are a bulldog.

CHAPTER 5

Establish a new regime—The bulldog mindset

Now that you have overthrown the regime or mindset of laziness and you've begun to replace it with the bulldog mindset, it's time to go deep. It's time to really establish your identity as a bulldog. This is where you really immerse yourself in all things that build a bulldog mindset and continue building your new identity, your new self-belief that you are a bulldog. Let's think about how our original mindset was built. Our laziness mindset was built over time and shaped by many external inputs such as the media, our parents, our peers, and other forces in our environment. We live in a world where we get so many messages that aim to tear us down and make us feel less than, not good enough, and just down right bad about ourselves. We must protect ourselves by controlling what goes into our minds, because what goes into our minds shapes who we are. What we consume, we become. When I was lazy, I watched TV, didn't read any books, played video games, and didn't take a real interest in personal development or controlling my external inputs. When I made the decision to stop being lazy and become a bulldog, I made another very important decision...the decision to turn off the TV and be very selective about the media I consumed. This was important because I needed to have the odds stacked in my favor. Watching TV was not helping me build or reinforce my new mindset. So, I decided to shut it off and start consuming media that reinforced my bulldog mindset and pushed me to do a lot of soul searching and character building. I started reading personal development books by authors like Ekhart Tole, Tony Robbins, Maxwell Maltz, and many others who have had a huge impact on how I transformed my life and my mindset. I subscribed to YouTube channels of like-minded people. I listened to audiobooks and subscribed to blogs that all reinforced what I was doing. One thing in particular that had a major impact on my life and was a real turning point for me in solidifying and expanding my bulldog mindset was an intensive 1-week Tony Robbins seminar called Date with Destiny. This seminar was life changing. Not only did it help me strengthen my bulldog mindset, it also helped me to clarify my vision. My vision of what was truly important to my life and the direction I wanted to go. I was able to clarify my passion and goals. I was inspired to make an even bigger impact than I was making. The experience also helped me to let go of being self-conscious and to just be myself and not give a shit anymore. I highly recommend an intensive experience like this that allows you to really connect with and further define the person you have decided to become. The beauty of this type of experience is that you will be around like minded people doing the same thing that you are and supporting you on your journey. You owe it to yourself and to everyone around you to find out who you truly are and to then unleash it. Life changing experiences are invaluable and support you in your journey of becoming a bulldog. Do some research and some soul searching. Really connect with your soul. Keep refining your mindset. And look for the best resources that will support you on your journey to become a bulldog. To help you with this, I have put together a free resource called The Bulldog's Playlist. In it, you will find a list of books, podcasts, and other resources to help you create a new, more empowering mindset. Get your free copy at https://simpleprogrammer.com/bulldog-playlist.

CHAPTER 6

Stand up, face your fears, and crush them

In order to be a fucking bulldog, you must face your fears and crush them. Dominating fear is key to being a fucking bulldog. This is at the heart of what makes you a conqueror. At the root of laziness is fear. When I was lazy, I was also filled with fear. So much so that I suffered from panic attacks. If you've ever had panic attacks, you know that they are one of the scariest things you could ever experience. I remember when I first experienced this. I was going to work and I started coughing. I felt like I couldn't get enough air. I expected it to go away but it didn't. It went on for an hour, then for 2 hours then 4 hours. I couldn't focus on work so I went home, I took a bath, and I tried doing everything I could to distract myself. They still didn't go away. I ended up going to a doctor who gave me a breathing test. After the test, the doctor told me that I should sign-up for the Olympics because I had the breathing capacity of an elite athlete. So clearly, there was nothing wrong with me and he told me that it was all in my mind. He offered to give me medicine for them, but I didn't want to take any drugs. Because these panic attacks were interfering with my life and were a threat to my livelihood, I knew I had to do something to get rid of them. I searched online for a cure and came across a video by a guy that gave some really good advice. He said that when you have panic attacks, instead of trying to avoid them, just experience it. Just face it. Really take it on and feel everything that's going on in your body while you are having a panic attack. When you do this, you'll realize that it isn't so bad and then you'll get over it. I was so desperate at this point, I gave it a shot. The next time I had a panic attack, I said okay, bring it! Give it to me. Give me everything you've got. The more I let myself experience it, the less I became afraid of it. It was like an instant cure. My panic attacks disappeared. Not only did this teach me how to get rid of panic attacks, it became a very valuable tool in helping me to overcome other fears I had. The reason I was having panic attacks in the first place was because I had let many fears fester within me without facing them or dealing with them. And when you let your fears fester and you don't deal with them, they will take over your life. I had developed a fear of roller coasters and a fear of flying. I faced both of these fears using the same technique, and overcame them. I now fly all around the world and I am not afraid of roller coasters. You can check out a video on my YouTube channel (https://simpleprogrammer.com/sbl-youtube) where you can see me overcoming my fear of rollercoasters. It is an incredible feeling when you are able to face your fears and crush them. What fears are you holding onto? What fears were at the base of your old mindset? Was it fear of rejection? Fear of failure? Dig deep and identify your fears. Once you identify them, do what I did and step into them. If you have a fear of rejection, step into it. What does it really feel like, mentally, emotionally and even physically to be rejected? What does it feel like to mentally, physically, and emotionally feel like a failure? Once you experience it, you'll realize it's not as bad as you think and then you can act, you can move forward, even while you're feeling this pain. You are no longer frozen in fear. You are showing this pain that it is not in control. You are showing your fears that you are the fucking bulldog, and they better step aside. When you're able to do this, know that you truly are now a bulldog.

CHAPTER 7

Obliterate the habits that are making you lazy

Aristotle once said, "We are what we repeatedly do. Excellence, then, is not an act but a habit." Our habits are very powerful because they are what we do REPEATEDLY. If you do something or neglect to do something every day, it becomes a part of you. Our habits have the power to move us forward or hold us back. They are at the heart of what makes us lazy. In order to stop being lazy, you must change your habits. You must delete habits that make you lazy and replace them with habits that will make you a bulldog. So, how do you obliterate the habits that are making you lazy? There are five steps you must take if you're really serious about changing your habits. The first step is to remember and to focus on your big vision. We talked about this at the beginning of chapter 4. Just like it's important to hold onto your vision when you are changing your mindset, it is just as important to hold onto your vision when you are trying to change your habits. Habits are hard to change. Your mind and body will fight you so it's really important to always remember why you are going through all the pain and discomfort. Your vision should be your anchor that keeps you going when the going gets tough. Now would be a good time to revisit your vision to make sure it is compelling enough to make you get back up when you fall and to make sure it's what you really want. If you need to tweak your vision to make it more appealing, now's the time to do it. The second step is a combination of commitment and decision. You must DECIDE that you want to eliminate the habits that were making you lazy and FULLY commit to eliminating them from your life. Just like you decided to become a fucking bulldog, you must decide to eliminate your old lazy habits. Once you've made this decision, it is critical that you fully commit. 100% and nothing less. You cannot, hesitate, fall back or leave yourself room to back out. If you hesitate, chances are you will fail and revert back to your old habits. When you fully commit to eliminating the habits that were making you lazy, you have the best chance of success. The third thing you need to do is to identify your lazy habits and choose new habits that will replace them. In order to get rid of habits that make you lazy, you've gotta know what they are. You've gotta call out your repeated actions that were making you lazy. After you've done this, you've gotta identify new habits that will make you a bulldog and support the new vision you have of yourself. Remember, you are what you repeatedly do. Since you are now a bulldog, your new habits must be the habits of a bulldog. It's not enough to act like a bulldog every now and then. If you wanna be a bulldog, you've gotta act like one all the damn time. Your habits must be the habits of a bulldog. The fourth thing you must do is to stop engaging in lazy habits. Just STOP. When I was lazy, one of my habits was eating a lot of junk food. When I decided to become a fucking bulldog, I stopped doing this. I had a vision of what I wanted to look like and what I wanted to feel like and I knew that eating junk food was not going to get me the results I wanted or get me closer to the person I wanted to become. So I stopped. The vision of who I wanted to become was so much stronger than my desire to eat junk food. The last thing you need to do to delete bad habits is to replace them with new habits. Habits of a bulldog. When I was lazy, not only did I eat a lot of junk food, I also did not have a fitness routine, so I gained weight. I got rid of my old lazy habit around fitness and I created a new one. I established a fitness routine and created new fitness habits of a fucking bulldog. To this day, I am in the habit of pushing myself and really challenging my physical limits. It's part of who I am and I wouldn't have it any other way. This is how you eliminate bad habits. Using your powerful, larger than life vision to drive you forward when the old lazy habits try to pull you back, you can eliminate those habits that were making you lazy and replace them with habits that transform you into a bulldog.

CHAPTER 8

Build a new kingdom—The environment of a bulldog

Let's face it. Becoming a fucking bulldog is hard. Because it is hard, your environment must support the new person you are becoming. Your environment can either make or break you, and at this point, you need to set yourself up for success. You must stack the odds of becoming a bulldog in your favor. Even with a changed mindset and changed habits, if your environment does not support you, or worse, goes against your efforts, you can very easily fall back into being lazy. So what do I mean by your environment? Your environment includes the physical space where you spend the most amount of your time. This includes your home, your car, and your office or workspace. Your environment also includes people you interact with. This includes family, friends, and co-workers. Now, you may not be able to control every single thing in your environment, but chances are, you can control or at the very least, influence most things. And remember, you want to set yourself up for success. You want to set yourself up for transforming into a bulldog. So ideally, your environment should trigger bulldog behaviors and feed a bulldog mindset. And at a very minimum, it should not trigger behaviors that make you lazy or put you into a lazy mindset. Let's start with things you can control. If the bulldog you has a vision of looking like an Olympic athlete or a fitness model, your environment should look as much as possible like that of an Olympic athlete or a fitness model. These athletes take their training and their diets very seriously. Their training and diets literally build their bodies. So, if you walked into their kitchens and opened up their cabinets and refrigerators, you won't find them filled with junk food. Instead, you will find foods that will nourish and strengthen their bodies and get them closer to their goals. This is what you want to do. If your refrigerator or kitchen cabinets have a lot of junk food, throw that shit out! Replace the junk food with foods that will give you energy and that are good for you. And if you live with other people who may not be on the same page, negotiate with them. Everything is negotiable. Ask them to take this journey with you or maybe do something like a 30-day no junk food in the kitchen challenge. You could make this something fun and it could give you enough time without this negative trigger in your environment to develop the habit of eating to support your new vision of yourself. And if this doesn't work, you may need to put yourself into a different and more supportive environment. Another very powerful trigger most people have in their environments is a television (or these days laptops and phones where media is consumed). There are tons of ads on TV, TV shows, and on the internet advertising foods that will not support you in looking like a bulldog. So what should you do? Turn it off! If you have that Frito Lay commercial playing in the background, it's going to make you want to get a bag of

Frito Lays. Again, if you don't live alone, negotiate to reduce the amount of time the TV is on or to only have channels on where the images and messages support you in building your vision. And again, if this doesn't work, you will need to consider getting yourself into a new and more supportive environment.

So how do you handle negative triggers from peers—family, friends, and co-workers— who are not on the same path as you? Those peers who'd rather sit around and watch TV than work out. Well, you have several options here. You could find a new peer group that has the same goals as you. There are a ton of fitness groups out there. For example, if running is your thing, you can join a 5k, 10k, or marathon training group. Many of these running groups have a social component, this could be a great way to expand your circle of friends and get the support you need to achieve your fitness goals. If you want to try something like Cross Fit, there are a ton of Cross Fit and boot camp style places around where you can train with a group of people with similar fitness goals as you. Another idea is to gather your friends and join a social athletic league. You and your friends can create a volleyball, basketball, or softball team. Doing something like this is a lot of fun and you're doing something with your current peer group that requires you to be active. So, there are always options. You can take the lead and influence a peer group to be a positive trigger for you in support of your fitness goals rather than going with the flow and allowing them to pull you back. If they're not open to this, you can change your peer group or reduce the amount of time you spend with them.

Take a really good look at your environment. If there are triggers that will pull you back into laziness, you need to get rid of them. Throw out the junk food, turn off the TV, change your peer groups, or change your peer groups…(that's not a typo either). As much as possible, create an environment that will support your vision.

CHAPTER 9

Build new muscles—Do hard shit

Now, if you really want to kick it up a notch where you crush laziness and transform your life beyond your wildest dreams, you must PROACTIVELY seek out and sign yourself up for mental and physical hardship. That's right. You have to proactively do hard shit. Proactively doing hard shit gets the bulldog mindset more deeply ingrained into your body, your mind, your heart, and your way of life. Remember when I said I don't wait for life to kick my ass, I kick my own ass? Well, I kick my own ass by doing hard shit. Hard shit that I don't fucking have to do, but that I make myself do to develop both mental and physical toughness. I don't wait for the challenges and pain that life will inevitably bring to make me mentally tough. By kicking my own ass and diving into pain that I choose, life's challenges seem easy in comparison to what I do to myself when they come. There's an old saying that goes, "that which doesn't kill you makes you stronger". And it's true. Pain and hardship, especially when you bring it upon yourself, builds character. And if the pain you pursue is physical, it gives you muscle and makes you physically stronger. There's another saying that goes, "Sweat more in training. Bleed less in war". Doing hard shit is your training. War comes when life throws you a curve ball. When those curve balls come, I'm ready

because doing hard shit before I'm required to puts me in a better position to survive and crush any pain or difficulties that curve balls bring. So, what kind of hard shit should you do? There are so many things you can do. The first place you can start is by doing some reflection to find out what you define as hard shit. Not just things that make you a little uncomfortable, but really hard things you just don't want to do. Keep in mind, you wanna make the hard shit you do productive. Any hard shit you pursue should contribute in some way to your overall growth as a fucking bulldog. I do a lot of physical hard shit. It's not uncommon for me to be in the middle of a 10 mile run and decide to go all out and run as fast as I can for as long as I can, purposely making my run even harder than it needs to be. I also do shit to run my business that's hard. I've written two really long books that have provided a ton of value to a lot of people. And both have been on best seller's lists. One book, *Soft Skills: The Software Developer's Life Manual (https://simpleprogrammer.com/sbl-soft-skills)* was 470 pages. My new book, *The Complete Software Developer's Career Guide,*
(https://simpleprogrammer.com/sbl-complete-software-developer) was 798 pages. Writing both books was very rewarding. HOWEVER, I'll be honest...the writing process is a bitch. It's really hard shit. The reason it's really hard is because during the process, which is a really long one in my case, you can and will get bored. You may experience writer's block, but you still have to complete the book despite this. The momentum that you start off with in your first few chapters is the momentum you must maintain throughout and that is

some hard shit. And that's just the writing process. Marketing a book is another task that is critical to the success of your book and is also really hard shit. I had to come up with a marketing and sales plan that would get the book into as many hands as possible. Again, hard shit. I chose to write and market my books because it was hard, and because it lines up with the vision I have for my life as a fucking bulldog. Bulldogs don't quit, no matter what. Bulldogs take action even when it's hard. My main goal with getting my message out through my books, blog, and videos is to inspire as many people as I can to be the best version of themselves. I tell people all the time to seek out and do hard shit and that hard shit will make them grow. The books that I've created are literally a product of that message. So for everything that was hard about writing my books, the level of grit I gained from the process and the end result of both books are priceless. When you pick your own hard shit to do, make sure that whatever you choose will help you grow in some way. If you need some inspiration, I have compiled a Hard Shit List. That's right. A lot of people walk around with shit lists that are of no use to anyone, but in this book, you've got a Hard Shit List to give you some inspiration and keep you going on the path to becoming a bulldog. You can find the Hard Shit List in The Bulldog's Playlist, the free resource you can download here (https://simpleprogrammer.com/bulldog-playlist).

CHAPTER 10

Don't start shit you can't finish— Become a finisher

Finishing shit you start is the only way to success. 50% done is worthless. 90% done is worthless and a big waste of time. You only get benefits from doing something when you reach 100%. When I made the decision to stop being lazy and become a bulldog, I also decided to become a finisher. Before making this decision, there were a ton of projects that I had started but never finished. When I made the decision to become a finisher, I was working on an app called PaceMaker. Pacemaker is an app that helps you run at a desired pace by telling you to speed up or slow down when you are running too fast or too slow. I put a ton of work into it and I even hired a designer to design the interface. When I was almost done with the project, I realized that I didn't know how I was going to implement it. This seemed like yet another hard task within this project. I found myself starting to lose interest and wanting to quit. At this point, I had invested a lot of time into building the app. As I thought about quitting, I also thought about the amount of time I had already spent working on it...time that I could never get back. And, I also thought about how I invested in getting a design built for it. When I really thought about everything I had already put into it, I was determined to figure out a way to just get the shit done. This is when I decided to become a finisher. I figured out how to implement the app and I launched it in the app store. This paid off big time. Finishing and launching this app got me on the news. I pitched it to Shape magazine and they ended up publishing a tip about it. Right after this, I got an explosion of sales. Finishing this project along with the work I had been doing on my blog led me to another opportunity with a company called Pluralsight (https://simpleprogrammer.com/sbl-pluralsight). Pluralsight publishes online video courses, mainly for software developers. They were looking for someone to teach a course in Android Development. The app I developed was an Android app and I had also written blog posts about Android. I ended up working with Pluralsight to develop this Android course. This one course was just the beginning. I ended up creating 55 courses for them. Again, this was no easy task. In order to create courses, I had to be a finisher. Creating these courses was fulfilling, but some of the work required was tedious and boring. I had to plow through all of the shit required to complete these courses whether I felt like it or not and whether or not the task was fun or boring. By taking action and finishing all these courses, I was able to prove to myself and to the world that I really am a finisher. So, how did I become a finisher of big projects with tedious tasks? It was a combination of things. I had a vision of the completed project. I made an all in, 100% commitment to get it done even when it was not fun. I created for myself real deadlines that I made myself stick to. And let's not forget, I had the tenacity of a fucking bulldog. Similar to the vision of the life you want to have and the type of person you want to become when building a bulldog mindset, you must have a vision for what your project will look like when you're done. If you don't have this, you don't have anything to get excited about. And you need this to hold onto when you get bored or tired of doing all the grunt work. You need to see what waits for you at the finish line. It helps when you are excited about your projects, but excitement will only get you so far. What will carry you across the finish line is commitment. 100% commitment. If you are not fully committed, you won't finish. What also pushes you across the finish line is a clear and solid deadline. If your project has no deadline, you'll never get it done. And last but not least, the fuel that will get you through the rough times is tenacity. This is where your bulldog mindset comes in. Remember, real bulldogs don't give up and they don't start something they can't finish. They never quit, no matter what. Use your bulldog mindset to make you a finisher.

CHAPTER 11

Defeat overwhelm—Learn how to feast on an elephant

One major contributor to laziness is overwhelm. When we have a ton of things on our plates, it's easy for us to look at them and say, "I could never get all that done." So we just procrastinate and let them sit. Procrastination makes the feeling of overwhelm even worse. The more you put something off, the bigger it grows in your mind and in reality. Overwhelm is one of the most popular excuses for being lazy. The remedy for this is to face it and then overcome it. The feeling of overwhelm is based on fear. Fear that the project or tasks at hand are bigger and more powerful than you. Remember in Chapter 6 where we talked about facing your fears and then crushing them? This is the same thing you must do with overwhelm. Face it and then crush it. Face overwhelm by sitting with this feeling and really feeling it. Don't try to avoid the discomfort of how it feels. When you do this, you will realize that it really isn't as bad as it seems. After you do this, really take a look at your projects or tasks. Then, remind yourself of your new vision of yourself as a fucking bulldog. Do your projects and tasks line up with the person you are transforming into? If the answer is no, toss 'em. There's no need to hold onto old shit that no longer serves you and won't get you closer to the person you want to become or having the lifestyle you want to have. The next thing you want to do is to prioritize your tasks and projects. You don't have to do everything, all at once, right now. You can prioritize your tasks and projects over a period of time so that you can focus on them and get them done. After you've prioritized, you need a plan and some tools to help you break down large tasks and projects into manageable chunks. How do you eat an elephant? One bite at a time. If you plan to feast on an elephant—eating more of it more quickly—you need the right techniques. One technique that I use to help me accomplish my elephant sized projects faster and more efficiently, is called the Pomodoro technique. The Pomodoro technique is a system where you plan your work in 25 minute increments and after 25 minutes of uninterrupted focused work, you give yourself a break. You plan out the number of Pomodori (plural for Pomodoro) you are committed to accomplishing for the day, for the week, or for longer periods by using a planner or calendar to assist you. The tool I use to plan and track my Pomodori is called Kanban Flow. One of the reasons I really like this tool because it has a built in Pomodoro timer. The reason this technique works so well is because it's easier to give a task your 100% undivided, uninterrupted attention than it is to give this same level of focus to something for, say a 3 hour time block. Using this technique is how you're able to complete huge projects and tasks...one Pomodoro at a time. You can set goals for how many Pomodori you will complete in a day, a week, etc. Looking at your work in this way, chunks it down into pieces you can see yourself completing instead of looking at it like a huge overwhelming project. Once you face the feeling of overwhelm and use a technique like the Pomodoro technique and then schedule and track it with a tool like Kanban Flow, you will see your productivity and the amount of things you get done skyrocket! You'll also find that your habit of procrastination will diminish. In The Bulldog's Playlist, the free companion resource you can download here (https://simpleprogrammer.com/bulldog-playlist), I provide you with more information on Kanban Flow and the Pomodoro technique.

CHAPTER 12

Life is a fucking adventure—Take risks

Let's face it. Life without risk is boring. It may be safe, but it's just fucking boring. And what good is that? When we're used to living in a state of laziness, we are playing small. We're hiding, not showing up for life, and not living up to our potential. Like overwhelm, avoiding risk is based on fear. Fear of failure, fear of rejection, or even fear of success. And as we've already learned, the only way to deal with fear is to face it and crush it. And even after you crush it, if you still feel afraid to take risks, do it anyway. This is where your bulldog mindset comes in. Just do it anyway. Find something meaningful, adventurous, with an element of risk, and just fucking do it. You only live once and you don't want to have any regrets. When I decided to stop being lazy and I faced my fears, I embraced risk. I started a blog and then started producing YouTube videos. By doing this, I was taking a risk. I had never done anything like it before, I was not nearly as outgoing as I am now, and I didn't know if anyone would even give a shit about what I had to say. Despite this, I didn't give up. I kept showing up, kept learning and growing, and eventually, I developed a loyal following. I found that there were people who cared what I had to say and found value in the content I was creating. My now business, Simple Programmer, has evolved into a thriving company with employees. One of the biggest risks you can take is becoming an entrepreneur. Entrepreneurship does not offer any guarantees. Businesses come and go all the time. But entrepreneurship is one of those risks that can have a big financial pay off if you can stick it out, if you have the right strategies, and if you have a solid customer base that finds enough value in what you offer and are willing to pay you.

There are all kinds of meaningful risks you could take in life. You just have to figure out what's right for you. I keep going back to this, but it is so important. The best place to start is with the vision of what you want out of life and the vision of the person you want to become. That bad ass version of yourself that you are transforming into, what kind of risk would he or she take? Is it a physical risk? Maybe the bulldog you wants to climb a mountain. If that's your thing, there are all kinds of training programs to do something like this. Learn what it takes to climb a mountain, prepare yourself for it, and just do it. Have you always wanted to fly an airplane? There are tons of pilot training programs out there. Just do it. Do you have some strong opinions about how to make the world a better place? This has to be one of the best times in history to get your message out to millions of people. The possibilities are endless. So Be BOLD! Dream BIG! DON'T LISTEN to reason because it is probably fear holding you back. Just fucking go for it. Take a risk. Life is too short to be boring.

Chapter 13

Go Public—Publically declare that you are now a bulldog and show ' em what you're made of

A really good way to hold yourself accountable and stay on track is to go public. Declare to the world, or at least your family and friends, that you have made the decision to become a bulldog and you are relentlessly pursuing a major life transformation. Why go public? Why not keep it a secret? Because if you publicly declare that you are about to do something life changing, the world will hold you accountable and cheer you on. Now, I didn't say everyone in the world would react this way. There are some people who want you to continue being a lazy ass. Some are haters, and others actually care about you and just don't want you to get hurt. This is all okay. The haters will fuel your determination to beat laziness even more. And your fans will give you encouragement to keep going when things get hard and you want to quit. They will also make you feel a greater sense of responsibility. If you don't follow-through on something or finish a big project that you've been talking about, they will ask you what happened and will be disappointed. Our actions not only affect our lives. They affect the lives of everyone around us. And when you become the person you want to become and get what you want out of life, you will inspire those around you. You're not beating laziness and becoming a bulldog for your benefit alone. You're becoming a bulldog for the world. And the opposite of this is also true. If you continue being lazy and not living up to your potential, the world and everyone around you will miss out on everything the bulldog you would have brought to life. And that would just be really sad. You owe it to yourself and the world to defeat laziness and unleash your highest potential. If I can do it, so can you. Most of my journey from laziness to bulldog is on YouTube

(https://simpleprogrammer.com/sbl-youtube) and in my blog (https://simpleprogrammer.com/sbl). I'm still growing so, if you subscribe to both, you'll see be able to see how far I've come and where I'm headed. If it's your thing, go public by sharing your journey on a blog or YouTube channel you create. If you like social media, talk about your journey on Facebook, Instagram, or some other platform. If you want to be more personal, share with those immediately around you off line. How you share doesn't matter. What matters is that you share and that you do not take this journey by yourself.

SECTION III

KEEP MOVING FORWARD

CHAPTER 14

Always be in constant pursuit of a better version of yourself

The journey from laziness to bulldog never ends. Ever. If you don't want to move back, you have to keep moving forward. You're either doing one or the other and there's no way around it. Think about it this way. You have more momentum when you're trying to climb a mountain than if you're trying to remain on a plateau. Climbing that mountain is a challenge. Real personal development and transformation is a challenge. There are always ways you can challenge yourself to be better than you were yesterday. So, even when you've gotten yourself out of laziness and achieved the lifestyle you want and become the person you want to be, there's always room for improvement. Keep raising the bar. You can never set it too high. As long as you are alive, there are greater things that you can accomplish and a greater person that you can become. I remember when I was overweight, I did a 90-day fitness challenge. I achieved my fitness goals and won the challenge, but then I got depressed. I was depressed because now that I had gotten to where I wanted to be, I didn't know where to go. I didn't know what was next. Once you have mastered laziness, you've got to know what comes next. For someone who has transformed themselves into a fucking bulldog, not continuing to grow and just staying in the same place is not an option. Throughout your journey, you must revisit the vision you have for your life. One of the questions you should ask yourself is, "what happens after my vision becomes a reality?" You want to have a plan in place for the next leg of your journey. You should even challenge your vision. When you created your vision, you still had the laziness mindset. Now that you're out of this mindset, can your vision of yourself and your life expand? Can you take this vision to new heights? Can you take your personal development to new depths? There is always a way to move forward. If you plan to be a bulldog and leave laziness behind for good, you must keep moving forward.

CHAPTER 15

Always remember why you stopped being lazy

I remember one day I was out doing one of my 10 mile runs after I had injured myself. I had been out for about 2 weeks because of this injury. This run was really hard because I was just getting back into the swing of things. During this run, my heart rate was much higher than it would normally be and I was struggling. It got so painful that I wanted to give up. All kinds of things were running through my mind. I started asking myself, "John, why the fuck are you doing this?" I said to myself, "You should just stop doing all this crazy shit and live a normal life. Just go and eat some pizza and just watch TV like a normal person." Then it hit me. I started to remember where I was and who I was before I went down this path. I had also injured myself several years ago and went through a crisis as a result. I had gained a ton of weight, and I was just lazy. During this time in my life, I was in a really dark place. I started thinking about just how far I had come. After really thinking about this, I was like," shit....if I quit and just give up now, I could fall back there. Back into that dark place where I was a lazy fucking person". The thought of going back there gave me a second wind. I sure as hell didn't want to go back to where I started. I had done too much work and had really developed my character to a point where I could not see going back. I literally started running away from my old self. I finished my 10 mile run and pushed through the discomfort because it was nothing compared to the painful place I was in when I was lazy. When you reach a low point on your journey out of laziness, remember the progress you've made and how far you've come. If you quit, you could go back to being that lazy person. And that is not what you want. Everyday, when it's easy and when it's hard, you must keep doing the hard shit that helped you to create your new mindset. You cannot give up. If you give up, you will end up right where you started.

CHAPTER 16

Never give up even when it hurts

Pain and never giving up have been major themes throughout this book. They will also be major themes in your journey out of laziness. Any major change we make in our lives will involve pain. If we really want to be different people, we have to be 100% committed to our transformations and there is pain and discomfort in any transformation process. As I talked about in Chapter 14, this process never ends. We should always be moving forward and wanting to make ourselves better. And this requires pain. When we proactively seek pain by doing hard shit, we become stronger and more resilient. There will be times you will want to give up, when you think it's not worth it. When you'll feel that the life you had when you were a lazy ass wasn't that bad. You'll be tempted to quit. But then ask yourself, "Would I rather feel the pain of what I am doing right now to help me grow or would I rather feel the nagging pain of laziness and mediocrity?" Growing pains are usually followed by rewards. The pain of mediocrity and laziness are usually accompanied with regret, guilt, or jealousy, especially when you see others embracing the pain of growth and getting all the benefits. So, never give up. Remember, you are a fucking bulldog now. Not a lazy ass. Bulldogs don't quit. They are tenacious and they get what they want out of life. The pain they endure builds muscles and character. Those are the real rewards. With this new character and strength, bulldogs can handle anything. If the physical things they build are taken away, they are still left with the new person they've become. They still have the strength, tenacity, and character to build something new. Even when it hurts, especially when it hurts, never give up. Love the pain. Lean into it. The pain you endure when you defeat laziness and become a bulldog is worth it.

SECTION IV

CONCLUSION & THE BULLDOG'S PLAYLIST

CHAPTER 17

Conclusion

Man, oh man. I can't believe we've made it to the end. Time flies when you're having fun. Thank-you for allowing me to share my experience with overcoming laziness. As I shared with you, when I was lazy, I experienced a lot of pain. The kind of pain that was of no use to me. When I decided to crush it, I still experienced a lot of pain, but this time, the pain brought big rewards with it. The rewards included me being a better person who experienced a lot of growth within a very short period of time. And, me being the person that accomplishes major goals and is able to contribute to the world in a much more impactful way that aligns with my purpose for being on this earth. Overcoming laziness is one of the biggest challenges people face today. It is also one of the biggest dream killers that exists. You are meant for greater things than you are currently expressing. Learn from my experience. When I stopped being lazy, the gifts and talents I brought to the world had so much more meaning and impact. You owe it to yourself and to the rest of the world to stop being lazy. We can benefit from your unique gifts...the gifts that only you can bring to the world.

Remember, you're not alone. I still do videos, write blog posts, and answer emails giving advice on how to stop being lazy. If you need support, subscribe to my blog (https://simpleprogrammer.com/sbl) and YouTube channel (https://simpleprogrammer.com/sbl-youtube)

I wish you much success on your journey. I hope that my experience and advice will help you defeat laziness and step into the journey of becoming the best version of yourself.

CHAPTER 18

Special Bonus: The Bulldog's Playlist

Every bulldog must have a playlist, a set of tools and resources to strengthen your new mindset and help you stay focused while on your journey to defeat laziness. This is a free resource that serves as a companion guide to this book. In it, you'll find a compilation of books, blogs, podcasts, and other tools to support you. Download your copy of The Bulldog's Playlist here:

(https://simpleprogrammer.com/bulldog-playlist)

Made in the USA
Columbia, SC
26 December 2019